IMAGES OF WAR

TANK WRECKS OF THE EASTERN FRONT 1941–1945

An all too familiar sight in the early days of the fighting on the Eastern Front – a tank in a hole.

IMAGES OF WAR

TANK WRECKS OF THE EASTERN FRONT 1941–1945

RARE PHOTOGRAPHS FROM WARTIME ARCHIVES

Anthony Tucker-Jones

Pen & Sword
MILITARY

First published in Great Britain in 2018 by
PEN & SWORD MILITARY
an imprint of
Pen & Sword Books Ltd,
47 Church Street,
Barnsley,
South Yorkshire
S70 2AS

ISBN 978 1 47389 500 3

A CIP record for this book is available from the British Library.

Typeset by CHIC GRAPHICS

Printed and bound by CPI Group (UK) Ltd, Croydon, CR0 4YY

Pen & Sword Aviation, Pen & Sword Family History, Pen & Sword Maritime, Pen & Sword Military, Pen & Sword Discovery, Wharncliffe Local History, Wharncliffe True Crime, Wharncliffe Transport, Pen and Sword Select, Pen and Sword Military Classics, Leo Cooper, The Praetorian Press, Remember When, Seaforth Publishing and Frontline Publishing.

For a complete list of Pen & Sword titles please contact
Pen & Sword Books Limited
47 Church Street, Barnsley, South Yorkshire, S70 2AS, England
E-mail: enquiries@pen-and-sword.co.uk
Website: www.pen-and-sword.co.uk

Contents

Introduction
To the Victor the Spoils

The war on the Eastern Front was one of the most appalling bloodbaths in military history. Study of the conflict shows that both sides had a propensity for photographing each other's destroyed and wrecked equipment – in particular tanks. Individual soldiers as well as dedicated propaganda units took a perverse delight in chronicling their victories by photographing the destruction and mayhem. Soldiers could simply not help themselves when it came to posing atop an enemy tank or inside the cockpit of a downed fighter plane. Such photographs, official or otherwise, were sent home to proud family members who were reassured that their loved ones were safe and on the road to victory.

The fundamental question is why are the Red Army's defeats of 1941 and 1942 so well photographed? How did Hitler with a force of around 3,500 panzers overwhelm Stalin's tank fleet of some 20,000? The truth of the matter is that by the time of Operation Barbarossa most of the Red Army's under armed and under armoured tank fleet was completely obsolete. To compound matters, the Red Army was in some disarray thanks to Stalin's purges and an ongoing reorganisation. Its training was poor as was the supply chain and logistical support. This of course was aggravated by the enormous size of the Soviet Union.

Crucially, Soviet tankers lacked adequate training at a tactical level, while their tanks were often short of ammunition and fuel. Reports indicate that around 30 per cent of Soviet tanks needed repairs before the war even started. Once the initial fighting commenced up to 50 per cent of the Red Army's tank fleet was simply lost to mechanical problems and a lack a fuel. In other words, gross mismanagement and incompetence. The Red Army high command saw it as such and many generals were executed as a result of this poor performance.

Technically, in some areas, Soviet tank design was superior to that of the German panzers. For example the T-26 light tank and BT-7 fast tank were both armed with a 45mm gun, which was larger than the standard German 37mm. However, both tanks had very thin armour and their tracks were too narrow to handle excessive off-road condictions. Likewise, the formidable KV-1 heavy tank and T-34 medium tank were armed with a 76.2mm gun, which was of an inferior velocity than originally intended, thanks to the obstructive political machinations of the Red Army's Artillery Directorate. Both, though, had thick sloped armour and wide tracks that spread the ground pressure giving them better cross-country capabilities than their opponents.

While the KV-1 and T-34 were very progressive designs with a good armament-armour-mobility ratio, both were let down by clutch and transmission problems. While the T-34 was eventually fine-tuned into a war-wining tank, the KV-1's automotive problems were never fully rectified and it was eventually dropped from production in favour of newer designs and self-propelled guns. Although well-armed when the war broke out, neither the KV-1 or T-34 were available in large numbers. Those in service were quickly lost thanks to incompetent crews. Some 75 per cent of the Soviet tank force comprised T-26s and BT-7s, and most of these were swiftly lost trying to defend the approaches to the Soviet Union's major cities.

At the point Hitler struck the Soviet Union the Red Army was in the middle of a major reorganisation and redeployment. Stalin's generals, in a bid to counter the growing Nazi menace, were in the process of moving reinforcements westward. His commanders struggled to agree over how best to use their tanks; should they support the infantry or be massed as a dedicated mobile reserve force. On the eve of war it was decided to organise dedicated mechanised corps, these though were far from ready.

Readers will note a discrepancy in the proportion of Soviet to German tank wrecks. There is a good reason for this. By 1943, in the face of mounting defeat, the Germans had largely stopped photographing knocked out enemy tanks – there was little propaganda value in it and to have done so was extremely dangerous without control of the battlefield. The Red Army by this stage largely had much better things to do. Only the powerful Tiger and Panther remained of much interest to them for intelligence and propaganda purposes.

At the start of the conflict on the Eastern Front there is a very visible trend with photographs of Soviet tank wrecks. Many were clearly undamaged and often abandoned in positions that indicated the crews fled their vehicles in panic. Stalin's tank forces simply dissolved when struck by Hitler's Blitzkrieg. Some, though, were battered and burnt out with charred crew members killed in and around their knocked out mounts.

Not only did both sides photograph each other's equipment, they also filmed it and put it on display. In the case of the Waffen-SS they set up a special company of war correspondents, or SS-Kriegsberichter, in early 1940. They were drawn from the flourishing German media industry, in particular camera men, photographers and radio commentators. At the start of the war they tended to accompany headquarters units, thereby keeping out of harm's way. It took them a while to learn their craft and the initial photographs taken during the invasion of France were rarely of the front lines and tended to be of a static snapshot quality. Most 'battle scenes' were posed and therefore fake.

Once in Russia the SS-Kriegsberichter took far greater risks by accompanying the advancing columns into contact with the Red Army. Reichsführer-SS Heinrich Himmler, who fully appreciated the value of Nazi propaganda, was not slow to encourage their work. The war correspondent company was expanded to a full battalion in August 1941 and then to a regiment in December 1943. At that stage their 'SS-KB-Abt' cuff-titles were replaced by a white on black armed band featuring the name 'Kurt Eggers'. This was to honour Eggers who had been killed at Kharkov while with the SS Panzer Corps. Many reporters wore both the cuff-title and the arm band. Some were also permitted to wear the unit insignia of whoever they were assigned to. These men took tens of thousands of photographs, but their work was not usually credited.

Tank wrecks were a very valuable source of intelligence. Once the Germans were in possession of the T-34 they were dismayed by its superiority. The Soviets immediately got hold of the German response to it. They obtained their first example of a destroyed Tiger tank on 21 September 1942. They secured a second disabled one on 14 January 1943. Examples of the Panther were captured as soon as it was deployed that summer at Kursk. The intelligence gained from them proved invaluable.

The German Army Weapons Officer at Kummersdorf instructed in 1940 that it was to be supplied samples of every captured enemy armoured vehicle. After they had been evaluated they were sent to the Tank Museum at Stettin-Altdamm for storage. Army Group Centre laid on an exhibition of captured Red Army equipment for the benefit of Adolf Hitler at Berlin's Zeughaus (the old armoury on Unter den Linden) on 21 March 1943. Ironically, it was used as cover for a failed attempt on Hitler's life. He seems to have taken little interest as he hastened through the exhibits without pausing, which saved his life. Likewise, the Red Army gathered captured panzers, which included Panthers, Tiger I and IIs, in Moscow and put them on public display. These had first been sent to Kubinka for technical evaluation.

* * *

Photograph Sources

All photographs in this book are sourced via the author.

Chapter One

T-26

The T-26 light tank constituted Stalin's most numerous tank type in 1941. It first entered service a decade earlier and by the time of the Second World War some 12,000 had been built. Essentially, there were four models of the T-26, the M1931, M1933, M1938 and M1939. The T-26 first saw combat in the Spanish Civil War, Russo-Japanese border conflicts and the Russo-Finnish War. The Red Army was also equipped with smaller numbers of the T-37, T-38 and T-40 light reconnaissance tanks.

In early 1931 the Revolutionary War Council took the decision to mass-produce the T-27 tankette, which signalled the Red Army's commitment to developing its armoured and mechanised units. At the same time it was decided to build the T-26 light tank. While the tiny two-man T-27 was intended to carry out reconnaissance work, the T-26 was to support the infantry divisions during the breakthrough of enemy lines. This formed part of the Red Army's developing concept of Deep Battle, which envisaged enveloping an enemy over a very wide area.

The T-26 was based on the British Vickers-Armstrong 6-ton Mk E light tank built for the export market. This came in two versions, the Type A and B, one with twin turrets side by side and the other with a large single turret. The first examples of these had arrived from Britain in 1930, but before they were put into production the Soviets produced competing prototypes known as the TMM-1 and TMM-2 with American engines and the driver to the left. The superior British design was then put into production under a licence agreement as the T-26 Model 1931. It was first seen in a large-scale display during the Red Square Parade on 7 November 1931.

The tank was powered by an eight-cylinder Armstrong-Siddeley petrol engine (known as the GAZ T-26), also produced under licence. This provided a road speed of 32km/h and a road range of 140km. The engine was located at the back of the hull with the transmission being sent forwards to the front drive sprockets. The gearbox located by the driver's feet had five forward speeds, and steering was of the clutch and brake type. The Soviet version retained the simple and robust Vickers suspension, which comprised two groups of four bogie wheels each side-sprung on quarter-elliptic leaf springs. The crew or fighting compartment was in the middle with the driver seated to the right of the turret.

The T-26 was initially armed with two DT 7.62mm machine guns mounted in twin turrets, though the T-26TU commander's variant was produced with a 37mm gun in the right turret and hand-rail frame antenna on the hull. It carried 180 rounds of main armament ammunition, had 3 crew and was normally issued to the platoon and company commanders. The Model 1932 also had a 37mm gun.

The initial double-turret configuration proved far from ideal. The gunners' seats did not automatically rotate with the turret mechanism, but had to be traversed manually, which was laborious in combat. In addition, to stop the turrets jamming each other locks had to be fitted to restrict traverse to 265 degrees.

As a result of these limitations the turrets were soon abandoned in favour of a single one. To start this was achieved by removing the right-hand turret and installing the gun in the remaining left-hand one. However, the German Rheinmetall 37mm gun chosen to up-gun the T-26 proved difficult to mount in the restricted space on the left. Firing this much more powerful gun generated a recoil that had a tendency to crack the turret ring.

Instead, the Bolshevik Leningrad Factory and the Kharkov Locomotive Works were tasked with developing a larger central cylindrical turret that could house the new 45mm Model 1932 gun. This became standard on the T-26 Model 1933 and on the BT-7 and T-35 tanks. Similarly, it was intended that all T-26s would have radios that required a distinctive horseshoe-shaped frame antenna fitted to the top of the turret. In reality, those tanks with radios were reserved for the platoon and company commanders. The horseshoe radio antenna soon proved vulnerable to artillery fire and was eventually discontinued.

The Model 1933 became the most numerous type of T-26 with over 5,000 being built by 1937. In service the crews soon developed an understandable dislike for the poor armour and the underpowered engine. Following the border clashes with the Japanese Army between 1934 and 1935, the T-26's riveted armour was dropped in favour of welded armour. This was after it was found that machine-gun fire split the rivets which then showered into the crew compartment. Attempts to improve the engine only managed to increase its 90bhp to 97bhp. The last of the Model 1933s built in 1936 were armed with two additional machine guns, one to go on the top of the turret for anti-aircraft duties and another one in the rear of the turret. It was followed by the Model 1938 and Model 1939 with a new conical turret.

A number of specialised variants of the T-26 were also produced, most notably the OT-26 flamethrower. This was based on the Model 1931 and had a flamegun mounted in the right turret with a range of 25m. To increase space for the fuel tanks the left-hand turret was omitted on the later versions. The turret, though, was simply too small for the flamegun so the larger Model 1932 turret was also used resulting in the OT-130.

This was followed by the OT-133 based on the more reliable and up-armoured T-26S. The OT-130 and the OT-133 saw combat during the Russo-Finnish War but their limited range made then vulnerable to enemy fire and mines. They lacked a close defence weapon as neither version featured a machine gun. These experiences led to the development of the KV and T-34 flamethrowing tanks. The OT tanks, though, were still in service in the summer of 1941. The Red Army also pioneered bridge-laying tanks, with the ST-26 seeing service between 1934 and 1938. It was fitted with a 7m bridge which could cross narrow gaps. Other variants included observation and towing vehicles.

The T-26 was blooded in the Spanish Civil War, 1936–9, the Russo-Japanese border war, 1938–9, and the Russo-Finnish War, 1939–40. The vast range of geography and climate conditions encountered meant that the T-26 was thoroughly tested. In Spain its Spanish Republican crews often lacked coordination with the infantry leaving the T-26 vulnerable to counterattack and artillery fire. Spanish Nationalist armour suffered from the same problem. However, throughout the war its 45mm gun gave it an advantage over Franco's Nationalist tanks and those of his German and Italian allies. The Nationalists were not averse to press-ganging the T-26 and offered a reward for each one captured.

Wilhelm Ritter von Thoma, who commanded the panzer training group in Spain, noted:

> Russian tanks began to arrive on the other side even quicker . . . They were of a heavier type than ours, which were only armed with machine guns [Panzer I], and I offered a reward of 500 pesetas for every one that was captured, as I was only too glad to covert then to my own use.

On 29 October 1936 Republican T-26s broke through Nationalist defences at Sesena, overrunning an artillery battery and destroying two tankettes. During the Red Army's fighting against the Japanese in the late 1930s the T-26 proved superior. In these campaigns the T-26 was deployed in mass with supporting arms such as infantry, artillery and bombers.

Nonetheless, the T-26's greatest weakness was its 15mm frontal and 6mm side armour. The use of new anti-tank weapons and indirect artillery fire during all three conflicts led to heavy losses. In Finland the lack of artillery and infantry support contributed to heavy casualties. It was clear that the T-26's days as an assault tank were limited.

As a result of these hard-won lessons the T-26 was redesigned leading to the final standard version, the T-26S Model 1939, known as the T-26C outside the Soviet Union. This had 25mm frontal armour and a new conical turret with thicker and sloping armour. The hull armour was also sloped and extra plates added. This made the tank heavier. Around 2,000 M1938/39 were produced.

Even so, by the time of Hitler's invasion of the Soviet Union in June 1941 the T-26 was obsolete when pitted against modern anti-tank guns. Production was stopped in 1940 with a view to replacing it with the T-34, which was just entering service. Although the 45mm gun could handle all German armour except for the Panzer IV, many T-26s proved mechanically unreliable. Most notably there were clutch and gearbox failures during the height of the fighting.

In the opening stages of Operation Barbarossa General Bogdanov's 30th Tank Division, equipped mainly with T-26s, counterattacked the 18th Panzer Division southeast of Brest Litvosk between 22 and 23 June 1941. It made no impression, suffering heavily at the hands of German anti-tank guns and dive-bombers. Poor crew training, lack of ammunition and fuel cannot have helped matters either. Afterwards his tanks lay wrecked and abandoned.

The crews quickly learned to loathe the petrol engine. Many of the T-26s photographed by the Germans were burnt out and surrounded by Soviet corpses. Often the crew, particularly the driver, caught fire along with their tank and were gunned down trying to escape. Other tanks were decapitated, either by direct hits or the ammunition 'cooking off'. Some had received hits to the driver's hatch, killing the unfortunate driver. Overall, the T-26, despite its large numbers, did nothing to help save the Red Army.

The early T-26 Model 1931 light tank was a licensed copy of the British Vickers 6-ton export tank.

These Model 1931s, lost fighting the Finns, are armed with a 37mm gun. This type is also sometimes referred to as the Model 1932, while the commander's variant, called the T-26TU, had a 37mm gun and radio hand-rail frame antenna on the hull.

This knocked out Model 1931 has only been fitted with a single turret. The front has been blown apart.

A German officer and solder inspecting a pristine T-26 Model 1933. This version has the single cylindrical turret armed with a 45mm tank gun. This is a radio tank and would have belonged to a platoon or company commander as the turret has the horseshoe hand-rail antenna (though part of it is missing). Note the two forward opening square turret hatches.

This tanker met a gruesome fate on the back of his highly flammable petrol-driven Model 1933. The turret's large overhanging rear is clearly visible. It appears to have a single-piece rectangular turret hatch.

The crew members of a T-26 Model 1933 who never managed to escape. In the mid-1930s some of these tanks were upgraded with the installation of a machine gun in the back of the turret which had a circular mounting.

Another stricken M1933, and a dead crewman laying just in front of his machine. On such an open landscape there was nowhere for tanks to hide.

Two abandoned M1933s, the nearest has the single-piece turret hatch.

These German soldiers found these M1933s with their rearward facing turrets at the roadside. It appears both broke down as their engine covers are raised. Tankers often drove with the turrets in this position.

The tank on the right has a late 1930s upgraded turret which appears to have a circular hatch and mounting for an anti-aircraft machine gun. For some reason the tanks are facing back to back.

This shot shows just how exposed the driver was with the double hatch in the open position. This large gaping hole was simply asking for trouble.

This Red Army column led by a T-26 Model 1933 was lost in an ambush in Finland. Tankers hated fighting in forests and urban areas.

Soviet infantry killed while riding on a Model 1939 with the newer conical turret fitted with sloped armoured plates. It has the machine-gun fitting in the rear of the turret, which was removed on some tanks.

Two of the crew of a radio tank Model 1939 have been taken prisoner. The third was killed while trying to escape over the back of his tank.

While the T-26 was supposed to offer support to Soviet infantry, once it had drawn enemy fire it often proved a death trap for them.

An M1933 is just visible in front of this M1939. The latter has been immobilised by enemy rounds which tore off the road wheels and tracks. The scorching at the rear indicates the engine caught fire. In desperation a panicked crew member sought sanctuary underneath his tank.

There is no sign of damage to this M1938/39 T-26 except that it has lost its left track while reversing. The body in the foreground is possibly a crewman.

This dramatic photograph taken on the road to Moscow shows the difference between the M1938/1939 conical turret and the cylindrical one on the M1933, in the background. The horrific charred remains of a crew member can be seen on the engine deck of the nearest tank.

This derelict M1938 or M1939 marks the resting place of three Soviet infantrymen.

Lost in combat – this T-26 illustrates how thin the hull side armour was. Two rounds easily penetrated the fighting compartment and severed the tracks. The commander was killed before he could escape and his body was incinerated.

The driver of the T-26 had one of the least enviable jobs. A hand is grim testimony to the fate of this tank's crew. Hopefully, death was instantaneous as the blast took off the turret and turret ring, however, this damage may have been a result of the ammunition cooking off and exploding.

Another shot of the T-26s lost defending Moscow. Corpses lie scattered in the snow.

This group of German sightseers does not seem put off by the gruesome remains of the T-26's crew. The inclusion of the heavy tow chain at the back of the tank suggests that tanks were called upon to help each other on a regular basis.

The same tank from the front with more casualties strewn on the ground.

The shattered remains of a T-26 caught in a cornfield. The platoon commander's tank is in front just to the left.

A blood-splattered M1939 – the men on the outside of the tank were either caught by German machine guns or shelling.

German passers-by ransack a M1939, like all soldiers they would take anything that was useful. Two of its crew have been placed at the roadside. The turret has some sort of tactical marking consisting of a horizontal white stripe.

While the sloping armour on the rear of the M1939 turret offered some deflection properties, the overhang inevitably created a highly dangerous shot trap.

A T-26 rests in silent watch over a Russian Orthodox church or monastery. As with most abandoned T-26s, the commander and loader's hatches have been left open. Here there is a combination of square and round ones.

The front of this M1938/39 turret shows how the side armour sloped into the tank's superstructure. This photograph also gives a clear impression of the running gear with the front sprocket, rear idler, four return rollers and the four twin bogies.

By the end of 1941 it was very apparent that the T-26 was completely obsolete and it did not fare well in the winter fighting.

A Model 1933 T-26 obstructing the tramlines in one of the Soviet Union's captured cities. The rear of the turret has been blown out.

Yet another T-26 abandoned at the roadside. This was a familiar sight on all the routes leading to Minsk, Smolensk, Moscow, Kharkov and Kiev.

Something inside this T-26 has caught the eye of these German soldiers. It might be a crewman but their lack of helmets suggests that the tank has been there for a while and is well behind German lines.

It is disturbing that most captured T-26s were surrounded by Soviet corpses, and this example is no exception. The tank itself seems intact.

These German soldiers are probably gathered round this T-26 Model 1939 for instructional purposes. Their towed 37mm anti-tank guns would have easily dealt with its thin armour.

A late model T-26 caught in the open. It would have been impossible to escape artillery fire or dive-bombers.

A decapitated T-26. Those tanks built after 1940 had a new type of turret ring. Around 2,000 Model 1938/39s were built.

After a roadside firefight, German troops pick through the debris left by the losers.

The victors pose with a T-26 and a toppled statue of Lenin. The T-26 was scheduled to be replaced by the T-34 and was not kept in production.

A field of captured Red Army armoured vehicles that includes a number of T-26s. The nearest has a unusual wavy line camouflage pattern applied to the turret and superstructure.

Chapter Two

BT-7

After the T-26 the other mainstay of the Red Army's tank fleet in 1941 was the Bistrokhodny Tank (or BT fast tank). It was known to the crews as Betka (Beetle) or Tri-Tankista (three-man tank). The idea behind a fast tank, as opposed to a light tank, was that it would have a mechanised cavalry role, with the T-28 medium tank in an infantry support role. However, by the late 1930s, because of the Red Army's continually evolving and changing attitude toward the use of tanks, they were all seen as infantry support weapons.

Ironically, the BT family of tanks came about thanks to an American design. During the 1900s, the Christie motor company had built civilian vehicles, but in 1919 constructed its first tank. Thanks to the lure of a potentially lucrative domestic and export market in 1928, J.W. Christie came up with a new tank. Despite its shortcomings, the US Army ordered seven Medium Tank T3 or Combat Car T1 in mid-1931. The resulting improved T-3E2 had a new two-man turret, thicker armour and five machine guns.

What made this design innovative was its simple solution to unreliable narrow tracks, which invariably had very short service lives. On the Christie tank the suspension used a track and wheel system. This meant it could drive minus tracks using just wheels to the front by road, then in about 15–30 minutes the tracks could be fitted to facilitate off-road combat.

This innovation came to the notice of Innokenti Andreyevich Khalepsky, who was in charge of the Red Army Military Technical Board. Moscow had systematically set up organisations in both the UK and US to acquire new military technology. In the UK the drawback was that the War Department only allowed the export of vehicles not being used by the British Army – hence the T-26. In the US the Soviet Amtorg Trading Company began looking at getting hold of the Christie tank.

The vice-president of Amtorg, A.V. Petrov, on 29 April 1930, signed a contract with Christie for two improved models of their tank. Amtorg negotiated a tough deal, essentially demanding exclusive rights to the tank for ten years, access to the technical drawings and the appointment of a Soviet engineer to work at the US

Wheel Track Layer Corporation. Preparations were then made to ship two Christie Model 1930 T3s to the Soviet Union.

Christie was not permitted by US law to export tanks to the Soviet Union because since the Russian Revolution it was a country that the US did not officially recognise. When the US State Department and the War Department got wind of the deal they attempted to stop it. Christie found a ready way round the problem, since the Soviets were only interested in the suspension system, the two vehicles had their turrets and main armament removed. On 24 December 1930 the two 'agricultural tractors' were shipped on their way.

Christie had no intention of being restricted by any exclusivity clauses and sold the design to the UK, France and Poland. Use of his suspension in the UK was to result in the poorly armed and armoured but fast family of cruiser tanks. The most famous being the Crusader, which saw extensive action in North Africa. When Christie died during the Second World War his company was tangled in lawsuits brought by the US government and facing bankruptcy.

Back in the Soviet Union the Kharkov Locomotive Works quickly set about building its own 10-ton version for evaluation, designated the BT-1 armed with machine guns in a small turret. This differed from the Christie design as it replaced the four solid twin-disc road wheels with spoked wheels. Notably, the first wheel was of a different style to the other three as it featured round holes between the spokes rather than the triangular gaps on the others.

Nonetheless the BT-1 retained the narrow tracks, characteristic American pointed nose or 'prow' on the front of the hull and the general layout. The driver was seated in the middle at the front and served by a central visor or hatch. The other two crew members consisted of the commander and gunner. Ironically, the Soviets seemed to ignore the fact that the Soviet Union's road network was extremely undeveloped, which largely negated the benefits of the track and wheel system. In addition, they must have known that ultimately narrow tracks were simply not suited to Russia's harsh winter conditions or the muddy spring and autumn.

The BT-2 armed with a 37mm gun or three machine guns entered service in 1932 and some were still active nine years later. This vehicle had a flat nose on the prow. It had the same road wheels as the BT-1 and the small one-man turret lacking a rear stowage bustle or bin. The machine-gun variant lacked fire power and proved unpopular with the crews so was dropped. Improvements to the BT-1 resulted in the BT-3 armed with a 45mm gun and solid disc road wheels. Not many of these were built and they ended up as bridge-layers or flamethrowers. Likewise, the BT-4 with a twin machine-gun turret was only developed as an unwanted prototype.

The BT-5 that went into mass-production in late 1932 was essentially an up-gunned BT-2 armed with a 45mm M1932 tank gun mounted in the larger cylindrical

T-26-style turret. The initial production run featured a very small rear turret bustle, but subsequently the model had a much larger one. Its V-12 petrol M-5 aero engine generated 350bhp and running on its tracks the BT-5 could manage 65km/h and on just wheels was even faster at 112km/h. It saw service in Spain, Finland and Mongolia.

Experience fighting the Japanese in Mongolia led to the BT-7 in 1935, which had thicker armour, increased fuel and ammunition storage and the T-26-style conical turret with ball-mounted machine gun in the turret. The BT-7's main armament was the M1935 45mm gun and could carry 146 rounds, which was much better than the BT-5, which carried anything from 72 to 115 rounds. It was powered by the new M-17-TV-12 petrol engine, which developed 500bhp. This gave a road speed of 72km/h and a cross-country one of 50km/h with a road range of 430km. The engine was a copy of a German BMW engine that had been developed for use with aeroplanes. On the BT-7 the maximum hull armour was increased from the 13mm on the BT-5 to 22mm, though the minimum remained the same at just 6mm.

The easiest way to tell the BT-7 and BT-5 apart was that the former had a rounded prow rather than the tapered but flat nose of the latter. In 1937 the BT-7 was produced with a cylindrical turret similar to that on the later T-26. However, it had two round hatches rather than the one round and one square configuration on the T-26. This version was followed two year later by the BT-7-2 which featured minor technical modifications. By 1939 the BT-7 was the main Soviet combat tank.

Inevitably, a number of support and special purpose variants were also produced. These included a close-support tank armed with a 76.2mm regimental howitzer, which required a larger turret, and was known as the BT-7A. A flamethrower version, which carried the flame fuel on the right-hand side of the hull in an armour pannier was called the OP-7. The commander's model was known as the BT-7(V) or BT-7TU, utilising the BT-5(V) turret with the radio frame antenna, although later models had the much less obvious whip or aerial antenna.

Just before Operation Barbarossa the Soviets produced a transitional tank that essentially paved the way for the war-winning T-34 medium tank design. This consisted of a much-modified BT-7, known as the BT-7M and BT-8 or Model 1938. At 14 tons, it was almost a ton heavier. The key change was that it had a sloping glacis plate rather than the rounded prow and a diesel engine. However, the armour was the same as the BT-7.

Importantly, the diesel engine reduced the risk of fire and increased the tank's radius by over 30 per cent for the same volume of fuel. It was simpler to produce and maintain. The V-12 liquid cooled engine was again courtesy of a foreign supplier and was based on the Hispano-Suiza 12Y designed for aircraft. This gave a top speed of 86km/h on the road and 50km/h cross-country.

Tank designer Mikhail Koshkin at Kharkov was not a fan of the wheel and tracks system, which he argued offered no real benefits in terms of the added weight. As a result, he worked hard to ensure that his new T-34 was not lumbered with it. Koshkin was also able to draw on the experimental BT-IS that had sloping side armour as well as a sloping glacis. Both features were to be incorporated into the T-34.

The BT-8 was armed with the newer M1938 45mm tank gun and could carry 146 tank rounds, plus 2,394 rounds for its 2 machine guns. Between 1939 and 1940 about 700 BT-7M/BT-8 were produced. These helped General Zhukov secure a decisive victory over the Japanese at Khalkhin-Gol in 1939. Nonetheless, BT-7 production ceased in 1940 with the introduction of the T-34.

Due to the numbers built, totalling about 7,000 BT-5/7, like the T-26, the BT series became one of the most photographed tanks following the German victories in 1941 and 1942. BT tanks were photographed in all sorts of predicaments, some were plainly abandoned, some burnout, others crashed into each other or stuck in swamps. Often, as with the T-26, it was the BT driver who failed to escape when the vehicle was hit.

An overturned BT-7 Model 1935 with the rounded hull nose and early cylindrical T-26-style turret. This tank caught fire, with the rubber tyres incinerated on the last three sets of wheels, while the outer one on the front is split.

A close-up of the same tank. Enemy fire has penetrated the front left mudguard and the side of the hull. The burnt remains of the driver are just visible in the open hatch.

Another overturned Model 1935 provides passing interest to a German infantry column. The front of the track guards are all bent out of shape.

This BT-5 seems to have crashed into a timber-framed building.

German troops trudge up a dusty road past a BT-7 Model 1935.

Souvenir hunters examine this second version of the BT-7. This is a Model 1937 with the newer conical turret. Note the 'Mickey Mouse'-style round turret hatches. The tank appears undamaged, although the right-hand side track guard is twisted out of shape.

Quite how this crash occurred is anyone's guess. The Model 1937 on the left running on just its wheels seems to have piled headlong into the other tank. It is equally possible that they were shunted together by passing panzers. On both the tyres have been turned to ash.

These BT-7 Model 1937s show no signs of damage. The two on the left have raised engine covers indicating they had broken down.

The large double driver's hatch left the driver horribly exposed when open. The churning water to the right of this tank suggests these Germans may have taken it for an unsuccessful test drive. Otherwise it is evidence of the panicked incompetence of the Soviet driver.

A smashed and mangled column which includes at least half a dozen BT-7s. The lead vehicle on the left has lost its turret.

Two German soldiers take the opportunity of posing with a BT-7 Model 1937.

Like so many BT-7s, these were en route somewhere before being abandoned at the roadside. The lead vehicle has thrown a track and been struck by a telegraph pole.

This flipped BT-7 illustrates how narrow its tracks were, making them comparable to those on the German panzers. It has experienced an internal explosion which has buckled the bottom hull plates..

One of hundreds if not thousands of BT drivers who died with their machines. The mantlet has been blown off and the tyres burned to ash.

At first glance this BT-7 was defending a hairpin bend rising up through the surrounding hills. On closer inspection the extended chain at the front of the hull means it was under tow before being abandoned to the passing enemy.

German horse-drawn wagons plod past two BT-7s. The tank had been intended to act in a cavalry role, but was too vulnerable.

Fire was always a tanker's enemy, as this burnt-out BT-7 shows. There was very little to tell the Model 1937 from the Model 1939 apart. Another tank in the background has lost it turret.

This BT-7 singularly failed to protect the infantry it was supporting. The darkened colour of their faces indicates they have been dead for some time.

Ultimately, many of the BT-7s, like the T-26s, proved to be little more than death traps. It has to be hoped that this unfortunate crewman was dead before his body was cremated. The nose of this tank was pierced just off to the right.

German troops examine captured BT-7s that were caught in an ambush. The nearest vehicle illustrates how exposed the horizontal exhausts were. These could be easily damaged by enemy small-arms fire and artillery.

Destroyed in a ripening cornfield, this BT-7 is missing its gun mantlet. The grave of a Soviet casualty poignantly rests in the foreground.

A BT-7 Model 1937 lost during the winter of 1941. It has been given a very basic coat of whitewash paint.

This looks to be a turret-less BT-5, some of which were used as armoured engineer vehicles.

A captured BT-7 Model 1935 in running-on-wheels configuration. Being able to drive without tracks was no great advantage in the Soviet Union where much of its road network was very rudimentary.

Chapter Three

T-28 and T-35

The T-28 medium and T-35 heavy tanks were only built in limited numbers, but like the T-26 and BT-7 proved a source of endless fascination for the German victors. The T-28 was one of the world's very first medium tanks, with about 500 of these and just 60 T-35s ever built. Due to its imposing size the T-35 was regularly captured on film. The T-28 for some reason is much rarer.

During the 1930s the multi-turret tank design was popular in the UK, France, Germany and the Soviet Union. While the idea of land-based battleships had its merits, only the Soviet Union saw such tanks go into action and they proved far from successful against the agile panzers with their better command and control.

Although designated a medium tank, the T-28 with three turrets looked more like a heavy tank and could be easily mistaken for the very similar looking T-35 heavy tank. It was developed as a breakthrough weapon at the Leningrad Kirov or Bolshevik Factory in 1932. It may have taken its inspiration from the British A6 medium and German Grosstraktor designs. The latter had been seen at Kazan when Stalin allowed the Germans to conduct secret tank training in the Soviet Union. Both countries, though, abandoned the multi-turret type tank as impractical. The British only built three A6s and the Germans produced just six prototypes of the Grosstraktor.

The T-28A was armed with a Model 27/32 76.2mm gun as its main armament but this was later replaced by the 76.2mm (L/16.5) gun. It was accepted as the Red Army's very first Soviet-built medium tank on 11 August 1933. It required a crew of six who manned the central turret with the main gun and three machine guns: a coaxial DT and two in forward-mounted turrets. It carried 70 rounds of main armament ammunition and 7,938 machine-gun rounds. In 1938 the L/16.5 calibre gun was upgraded with a 26 calibre L-10 and this was known as the T-28 Ob.1938 or T-28B.

Maximum armour was 80mm while minimum was 20mm. Although it was bulky and at 31.5 tons was three times the weight of the T-26 and BT-7, it was fast for the period managing 37km/h on roads. However, cross-country it was only capable of 20km/h. The T-28 was powered by a M-17L V-12 372kW (500bhp) petrol engine which produced 1,400rpm (this was a Soviet version of the American Liberty aero engine). The tank had a multi-wheel suspension with twelve wheels mounted in pairs either side. The drive sprockets were to the rear and the idlers at the front. Four return rollers were also fitted either side. Most of the suspension was protected by skirting plates that featured mud chutes to prevent clogging.

When the T-28 went into production it was built by the Red Putilov Factory in Leningrad as the Bolshevik Factory was busy producing the T-26. The first ten were ready to take part in the Moscow May Day parade in 1933. During its production run to 1940 the tank underwent four main modifications. The T-28A Model 1934 had a modified suspension that consisted of the twelve bogie rollers with four return rollers, plus increased frontal armour. The Germans dubbed it the T-28V, while the B version or Model 1938 was known as the T-28M. The main difference with the latter was that the main gun was uprated and a ball-mounted machine gun was installed in the rear of the turret.

When the Russo-Finnish, or Winter War, broke out with Finland, the Red Army had available the 10th and 20th Tank Brigades equipped with the T-28. The Finns soon nicknamed it 'The Mail Train' and although they had few anti-tank guns, they were still able to inflict heavy losses. The Red Army's response was to order the T-28C modification, with its frontal armour on the hull and turret boosted from 50mm to 80mm and the rear and side to 40mm with the use of additional 'screened armour'. Thanks to this increased protection the T-28 served in the breakthrough attacks against the Finns' Mannerheim Line in 1940.

The T-28 was intended for frontal assaults and as a breakthrough tank, hence the three turrets which could pour fire onto anything in its path. In 1941 when it came up against the panzers its auxiliary turrets were all but useless in open tank warfare. In addition, the tank's relatively thin rear and side armour plus its high profile made it an easy prey for enemy artillery, dive-bombers and tanks. In anticipation of the T-34, the production of the T-28 ceased.

During the inter-war years the Soviets had designed a series of Direct Infantry Support (NPP) and Distant Remote (DPP) heavy tanks which were underpinned by the Red Army's Field Regulations of 1929. Only the Soviet Union's massive industrialisation made this possible thanks to the provision of new factories capable of such an undertaking.

In December 1930 the Soviet Directorate of Mechanisation and Motorisation, in cooperation with the General Design Bureau of the Artillery Department, instigated the first heavy tank. The T-30 was envisaged as a 50-ton tank armed with a 76.2mm gun and five machine guns. A prototype appeared in 1932 but problems with the running gear led to the project being cancelled.

In Leningrad the Bolshevik Factory, with the assistance of German designers, came up with the 30-ton T-22 and T-29 armed with 76.2mm and 37mm guns. They also conceived the T-42 which would have weighed 100 tons and been armed with a 107mm howitzer. However, none of these designs went any further than the drawing board. These efforts may have been informed by German work on the Grosstraktor and the subsequent Neubaufahrzeug, though both these were medium tanks in the 20-ton range.

At the same time a second team was working on the T-35 and two prototypes were completed between 1932 and 1933. The T-35-1 weighed 50 tons and was armed with a 76.2mm based on the model 27/32 howitzer surrounded by four smaller auxiliary turrets, two with 37mm guns and two with machine guns. The front right and rear left mounted the heavier guns. It soon became apparent that this prototype was not suitable for mass-production.

The T-35-2 had a more powerful M-17 engine with a rebuilt suspension, fewer turrets and a crew of seven rather than ten. The armour was slightly thicker with 35mm on the front and 25mm on the sides, which could withstand shell splinters and small-arms fire. On 11 August 1933 the Work Defence Council authorised production of the T-35A, which required an eleven-man crew, at the Kharkov Locomotive Factory.

The T-35 was undoubtedly influenced by British and German designs, particularly the British Vickers A-6 Independent tank. Whatever its origins, the size and complexity of the T-35 resulted in only about sixty ever being built between 1933 and 1939. Like most early Soviet tanks, it suffered from poor quality control and assembly. Also it had inadequate steering which made it hard to manoeuvre. The Red Army needed large numbers of tanks quickly so the T-35 suffered at the expense of the BT fast-tank production.

Like all tanks, the T-35 went through endless fine tuning. The 1935 model was longer and fitted with the turret designed for the T-28 armed with the L-10 76.2mm gun. The 45mm gun intended for the T-26 and BT-5 tanks replaced the 37mm guns in the two sub-turrets. A final batch of six tanks had turrets with sloped armour.

The T-35 was issued to just three battalions of the 5th Separate Heavy Tank Brigade, which came under the Supreme Command reserve. A few were used in Finland to little effect. In the run-up to the Second World War it saw little active service and in 1940 at a conference of Red Army tank specialists it was recommended that the T-35 was relegated to training duties. Up to that point it only ever appeared during Moscow's May Day and November parades, where to the general public it looked a very formidable beast. However, it was decided to keep them in service until worn out.

When Hitler invaded, many of the operational T-35 were simply overrun by the panzers. Those serving with the 67th and 68th Tank Regiments forming the 34th Tank

Division, assigned to the 8th Mechanised Corps, quickly broke down during the battles that summer. Under noisy combat conditions with the engine running, trying to coordinate the actions of the dozen crew members proved almost impossible. A few remaining T-35s took part in the defence of Moscow by acting as fixed strongpoints.

Due to their impressive size the T-28 and in particular the T-35 proved a source of interest to the all-conquering Wehrmacht. Members of the army and Luftwaffe could not resist being photographed in front of the imposing bulk of these tanks. As a result, numerous photographs have emerged of the T-35, most of which were clearly abandoned having broken down. Some, though, were photographed on fire or with their turrets blown off. One T-35 pictured having thrown a track was under tow before its rescuers gave up.

An abandoned T-28B Model 1938 medium tank bearing the skull and crossbones. The main turret is reversed, facing rearward. This photograph gives a clear view of the rear drive sprocket and front idler along with the four return rollers.

This T-28B has its main turret facing backwards showing the rear-mounted machine gun. The weapons for the forward-facing machine-gun turrets are missing.

A burning T-28 with horseshoe radio antenna. The Finns nicknamed this bulky looking tank 'The Mail Train'.

A German Panzer 38(t) passing a T-28 radio tank fitted with the horseshoe antenna. Only about 500 T-28s were built in the late 1930s and it is doubtful many were operational in 1941.

A T-28 abandoned by the roadside.

Panzertruppen pose on a broken down T-28.

A T-28A Model 1934 armed with the initial 76.2mm KT obr, 1927/32 gun adapted from a regimental field gun.

A close-up of the T-28 suspension with the skirting plates removed.

A captured T-35A Model 1935 Tyazholy Tank, or heavy tank, showing the turret configuration, with the main T-28-style turret armed with a 76.2mm gun, two lower (one front and one rear) BT/T-26 turrets with 45mm guns, plus two machine-gun turrets (also one front and rear).

A slightly later captured T-35A Model 1938 fitted with the horseshoe radio antenna. Although an impressive looking monster with a maximum armour thickness of 30mm and a minimum of 10mm, it could be pierced by most anti-tank guns.

Not suitable for off-roading. At 50 tons it is not surprising that this T-35 became stranded in the mud.

This T-35 got itself stuck in an anti-tank ditch and with no way of recovery the crew abandoned ship. The Germans are dwarfed by its enormous bulk.

Just behind a T-26 light tank another T-35 lies abandoned unceremoniously in a ditch.

From the mud splattered up the side of this T-35, it would seem it managed to travel some distance before breaking down.

German infantry file past the rear of a T-35 obstructing the road. No signs of damage are visible.

A second T-35, possibly on the same stretch of road. This one is on the verge and was under tow at some stage.

German soldiers posing with a T-35 that has had its main turret blown off. This heavy tank was vulnerable to panzers, artillery and dive-bombers.

Rear view of the same tank. Both the back 45mm gun and machine-gun turrets have come off as well as the main one.

Some effort has been made to camouflage this T-35 with foliage. Like many others, it has been abandoned at the roadside, probably after mechanical failure.

A T-35 with its front turrets missing and the main one damaged.

It is easy to imagine what these Germans are saying – what a formidable tank but completely unwieldy. A few survived the German invasion to take part in the defence of Moscow.

Chapter Four

KV-1

The KV-1 heavy tank was just coming into service in 1941. Armed with a 76.2mm gun, it was both better armed and armoured than its predecessors, but was not manoeuvrable or reliable enough. About 5,200 various KV variants were produced and it remained in production until 1943. Its swansong was at the Battle of Kursk.

Soviet experiences in Spain demonstrated that the basic requirement of making tanks able to withstand machine-gun fire and artillery shrapnel was no longer sufficient. Although tank losses to direct fire were minimal, the emergence of new 37mm anti-tank guns and large-calibre field guns showed the way things were going. In response, in 1937 the Directorate of Armed Forces issued specifications for a new heavy tank. This would be able to act as a breakthrough weapon and engage enemy armour at the same time. This was to be able to resist up to 76.2mm guns out to 1,200m and be powered by a less flammable diesel engine.

Initially drawing on the multi-turreted T-35 heavy tank, it was proposed that this new tank would have five turrets. In light of the difficulties in coordinating the gunners, the designer got the number reduced to three with the main one armed with a 76.2mm gun and the two subsidiary ones armed with 45mm guns.

The Kharkov Locomotive Factory, having built the T-35, seemed the logical home for a new heavy tank. Stalin's purges had led to a shortage of engineers and the work was passed over to the Experimental Design Mechanical Section (OKMO) at the Bolshevik Factory in Leningrad, under N. Barykov, and the Zirovskiy Factory, led by Lieutenant Colonel Zh. Kotin. The latter was to prove particularly able and ultimately was to be responsible for the powerful late-war Joseph (Iosef) Stalin tanks.

In the spring of 1939 Barykov's team presented their ideas for the T-100 and Kotin's the SMK (named after the late Bolshevik leader S.M. Kirov). Both designs featured three turrets, and rather than use the T-35's dated and less-effective spring suspension, they used the new torsion bar suspension. They also had wide tracks to lower ground pressure and improved cross-country performance.

When Kotin argued with 'The Boss' over the futility of having three turrets, Stalin broke a turret off the presentation model saying, 'Why make a tank into a department store?' Both teams were then sent away to work on two turret prototypes. These were ready by the summer of 1939 and sent to the testing grounds at Kubinka outside Moscow. Kotin would not let the turret issue rest and in February started designing a single-turret version of the SMK. In August the plans were shown to Stalin and permission was granted for a third heavy tank prototype known as the KV (cravenly named after Marshal Klimenti Voroshilov – though it had been planned to call it the KS or Kotin-Stalin).

During the prototype trials held in front of Voroshilov the tank bearing his initials performed the best. All three were then packed off to take part in the Russo-Finnish War of 1939–40 with the 91st Tank Battalion, part of the 20th Heavy Tank Brigade. This seemed foolish as it exposed them to the risk of capture. They saw action between 17 and 19 December 1939 near Summa, supported by T-28s. The SMK was disabled after running over a mine and when its crew repaired the damaged track they could not get the engine started. Attempts to tow it with the T-100 failed. The SMK had to be abandoned and was not recovered until February 1940. In the meantime, on 19 December 1939 it was decided to put the KV-1 Model 1939 into production, of which just 141 were built.

It had been hoped to arm the tank with the F-32 76.2mm gun but problems ensured the turret was fitted with the much more inadequate short L-11 76.2mm instead. The T-34 was to suffer exactly the same problem thanks to the obstinacy of Marshal Grigory Ivanovich Kulik, head of the Main Artillery Directorate responsible for the gun factories. He was not a fan of tanks and refused to step up production of the F-32 and the newer F-34. His actions also ensured that there was a shortage of 76.2mm ammunition. Bizarrely, the T-34 medium tank would end up with a more powerful gun than the KV-1 heavy tank.

Use of the L-11 meant it had a distinctive mantlet due to the location of a recuperator above the barrel. Close protection on the KV-1was supplied by three machine guns; one coaxial, one in the rear of the turret and the other in the front of the hull (the M1939 does not seem to have had a hull machine gun but was fitted with a pistol port). The turret and hull front were protected by 90mm and 75mm of armour respectively, making it impervious to most weapons except at point-blank range. The KV-1 took a crew of five.

Although weighing in at 43 tons, it could still achieve 35km/h on roads and 13km/h cross-country. By road it could manage a range of 160km and across country 100km. This was thanks to revising the SMK suspension, which employed six wheels either side mounted independently on torsion bars with three return rollers plus wide tracks. The KV-1 was powered by a model V-2K, V-12 diesel engine generating 500bhp.

The KV-1's combination of firepower, armour and mobility made it one of the most powerful tanks of its day and was only rivalled by the T-34, which was under development. It seemed as if that along with the latter the KV-1 would give the Red Army the tools it needed to implement its theories of Deep Operations. While the KV-1 was very impressive in appearance and on paper, it paid a heavy price thanks to its weight. This meant that the KV-1 went into production despite a series of very serious problems that would be very detrimental to its combat performance.

Key among these was its antiquated transmission, as well as the clutch being difficult to operate. Alarmingly, the driver had to bring his vehicle to a halt to change gear, this prevented changing up through the gearbox while on the move to achieve any sensible acceleration. Likewise, it meant it was inadvisable to change gear while in combat as a stationary tank always offers a ready target. Engine efficiency was impeded by poor air filters. All this meant that the tank was difficult and exhausting to steer. In practice the mighty KV-1 breakthrough tank was impeded by poor mobility.

Visibility was not good either. With the tank closed up the commander and driver had limited vision. The design of the driver's periscope was poor as it only had limited traverse. Likewise, the quality of the laminated glass in the driver's forward slit visor was such that it was hard to see through. This often left him reliant on directions from the commander for the simplest of manoeuvres. In contrast, the commander had two reasonably good periscopes in the turret roof, but as well as coordinating the driver, gunner and radio operator, he had to double up as the gun loader.

Until 1943, when production was ended, the tank was subject to constant fine-tuning. Notably, the Model 1940 (German designation KV-1A), the main production model by the time of Hitler's invasion, was given a more powerful engine and the higher velocity F-32 gun, as originally intended. The latter had a new-style mantlet.

Kulik convinced himself and Stalin that the panzers were armed with very large-calibre guns and that Soviet tanks should be up-armoured. As a result 35mm armour plates were bolted onto the turret and hull, which were eventually superseded by stronger welded turrets. The bolt heads were very prominent on the turret sides. The M1940 with additional bolt-on appliqué armour was also known as the KV-1E.

KV-1 production was carried out at the Kirov Factory in Leningrad, but once the city came under siege by the Germans it was transferred to the Chelyabinsk Tractor Factory. There the design was simplified in the same way as was done with the T-34. Hull appliqué armour was standardised and simplified. A cast turret was introduced, which was easier to produce than the welded design, and the road wheels were simplified. This resulted in the KV-1B with a distinctive curved bustle that was cast as part of the turret. The shot trap created by the turret's rear overhand was also eliminated. Introduced in later 1941, it had its armament supplemented by a hull machine gun. The Model 1941 (KV-1B) was armed with the longer barrelled ZiS-5 76.2mm gun, which was very similar to the F-34 used in the T-34/76 medium tank. It was much more powerful than the F-32 and ended the illogical disparity between the Red Army's heavy and medium tanks.

The up-armouring of the Model 1942 (KV-1C), was carried out by Kotin's TsKB-2 (Central Design Bureau). The hull protection was increased from 75mm to 90mm, plus a new thicker cast turret with 120mm at the front was produced. This process of adding yet more weight caused more problems with the engine and transmission and the crews found the Model 1942 a mixed blessing. Also, by this stage the 76.2mm gun in both the KV-1 and T-34 was no longer really adequate.

KV-1s were photographed by the Germans in an array of different states. More than often they were intact, but some had experienced an internal explosion sufficient to blow the heavy turret clean off. This was usually as a result of ammunition 'cooking off'. Whatever its fate, the KV-1 always looked an impressive tank even when it was alongside the Tiger.

A good example of the first production model of the KV-1 designated the Model 1939. It is easily recognisable by the rounded recuperator above the 76.2mm L-11 tank gun barrel. The Model 1940 T-34 had a similar arrangement. The muzzle appears to be plugged, which was probably done after the crew were forced to leave their broken down vehicle. The M1939 lacked a hull machine gun but instead was fitted with a crude pistol port.

This KV-1 has got itself in a bomb crater and was photographed by passing German troops. It is unclear why the main gun is pointed skyward unless it was being used for indirect fire. This has the new-style mantlet for the F-32 gun.

Another view of the same tank. It is possible that it was dug in so it could fight 'hull-down' but for the amount of effort required it seems unlikely.

German infantry stream past a decapitated KV-1. In principle it was a good design but on the battlefield proved otherwise.

A German solder clambers over a KV-1 left stranded in the mud and ice. The right-hand side of the tank has been damaged. The KV-1 suffered from clutch and transmission problems, also it had to be brought to a halt to change gear.

The Model 1940 was the most common type of KV-1 at the time of Hitler's invasion. Like the previous example, this one seems to have got stuck in a bomb crater.

This tank appears to have been lost in combat, and the engine cover is lifted at the back suggesting an engine fire. The hull machine-gun ball mounting has blown out.

The turret of the Model 1940 KV-1 was up-armoured with 35mm plates which were bolted on. This inevitably added to the weight and put a greater strain on the engine and transmission. The Germans dubbed this version the KV-1E. The driver's periscope is above and to the right of the driver's vision port.

German soldiers examine the remains of a KV-1 that was hiding in the woods. It has the up-armoured turret which has done nothing to save the tank from destruction.

This grainy shot illustrates the shot trap created by the overhang on the back of the KV-1 turret. This was remedied on the Model 1941, which had a cast turret that all but eliminated the overhang.

Littering the landscape, this KV-1 was reduced to a pile of scrap metal.

Both the T-34 medium tank in the foreground and the KV-1 behind came into service in 1940. They are badly damaged and the lack of craters suggests that this was as a result of anti-tank gunfire.

Minus its tracks, this KV-1 has also lost its turret ring and the turret. The latter is upside down to the right of the image.

Dusty German infantrymen prepare to pose on a KV-1 found at the roadside. The enthusiastic cameraman caught them before they were ready.

Another tank driver whose vehicle became his tomb. The rounded edges on the front of the turret either side of the mantlet indicate it was cast rather than welded.

The early KV1s had a large shot trap at the back of the turret that could flick an incoming round into the turret ring, creating such an effect as seen here.

A Tiger I sheltering behind the bulk of a KV-1S – this version was designed to be lighter and faster.

An abandoned KV-1 with added turret appliqué armour.

An early Model 1940, the turret of which has received some punishment. The left side track is broken and the tow cable has been deployed.

Chapter Five

KV-2

The KV-2 heavy assault tank or artillery tank was armed with a massive 152mm howitzer. Despite the size of its gun, once again this tank was not agile enough and was regularly photographed by the Germans having been abandoned. Thanks to the Russo-Finnish War it was decided to develop an artillery support variant of the KV-1. The Finns, well dug-in along the Mannerheim Line, had shown that Soviet tanks were not suited for bunker busting. General Meretskov, commanding the Soviet 7th Army in Finland, requested a heavy tank mounting a large-calibre gun to deal with enemy fortifications as soon as possible.

The OKMO team, using its T-100 heavy tank hull, sought to arm it with a 130mm B-13 naval gun. This was quickly rejected because of difficulties accessing the navy's heavy weaponry and ammunition, which included semi-armour piercing rounds. Besides, using Kotin's KV chassis seemed a far more logical step from a production point of view.

The first attempts employing a lengthened KV hull to carry a 152mm BR-2 and a 203mm B-4 howitzer were not successful. The third design envisaged mounting a standard 152mm M1938/1940 L20 howitzer on an unmodified chassis. It was this that became the KV-2. The first trials took place on 10 February 1940 and thereafter two prototypes were hurriedly despatched to Finland's Karelian Isthmus. It is not clear if they were used in active operations or simply tested on captured positions.

The most immediate drawback with the KV-2 was very self-evident. The turret required to house the large 152mm gun was simply enormous and weighed some 12 tons. This meant that the KV-2 had a towering height of 4.9m compared to the KV-1's 3.1m. To protect this very exposed turret it was given 110mm frontal and 75mm side armour. This resulted in an overall weight of 53 tons compared with the 43 tons of the KV-1. This made the tank impervious to direct fire except at very close range by high-velocity weapons. The size and the shape of the turret inevitably led to its six-man crew dubbing it the 'Dreadnought.'

The clutch and transmission problems suffered by the KV-1 were greatly magnified with the much heavier KV-2, which used an unimproved 500bhp V-2 diesel engine. On a good day it could managed 25km/h on the roads and half that cross-country. The enormous weight of the turret and the poorly designed turret bearings meant the tank had to be on flat ground in order to traverse the main gun. Nor could the gun be fired while on the move. These limitations were not conducive for mobile warfare and confined the KV-2 to operating on the roads. By the time of the German invasion its original purpose as a bunker buster had become an irrelevance. Essentially, the KV-2 was consigned to the role of a mobile pillbox in the face of Operation Barbarossa.

The Germans soon discovered the only way they could deal with the KV-2 was by shooting off its tracks or wheels, thereby forcing the crew to abandon ship. An impressed Marshal K.K. Rokossovsky wrote: 'The KV tanks literally stunned the enemy. They withstood the fire of every type of gun that the German panzers were armed with. But what a sight they were returning from combat. Their armour was pock-marked all over and sometimes even their barrels were pierced.'

The 1st Panzer Division invading Lithuania hit a KV-2 using 50mm and 75mm guns more than seventy times but failed to penetrate the armour. Its continued resistance was clearly testimony to the bravery of the crew. Whenever a tank was immobilised artillery and satchel charges had to be used to finish it off. Unsurprisingly, most of the KV-2 losses in 1941 were due to mechanical problems or lack of fuel. For example, the 41st Tank Division had thirty-three KV-2s in its inventory, of which two-thirds were lost, just five to enemy action. By July 1941 the Red Army had 500 KV-1s and KV-2s remaining.

That October production of the KV-2 was stopped when Stalin's weapons factories were evacuated eastward. By that stage only 334 had been produced. Subsequently, a few were used in the defence of Moscow and Stalingrad. Use of the 152mm gun was not abandoned but was instead married to a turret-less KV chassis to produce the ISU-152 assault gun, which appeared in the summer of 1943.

There were a number of other KV variants. The most noteworthy was the KV-8 heavy flamethrower. The Russo-Finnish War highlighted the vulnerability of light tanks converted to a flamethrower role. In order to make space for the ATO-41 flamethrower (which was also installed in the T-34 to create the OT-34), the 76.2mm gun was replaced by the smaller 45mm. To conceal the barrel of the flamegun it was camouflaged with a gun jacket. The KV-8 had enough flame fuel for 107 shots and could fire 3 shots every 10 seconds. These tanks were organised into flamethrower battalions comprising two companies of KV-8s and one company of OT-34s. Once all the KV-8s were lost in action they were phased out.

It was planned to create a KV-3 at Kirov armed with a 107mm gun using a longer hull and larger turret, but this was shelved in favour of using the prototype chassis armed with an 85mm naval gun for the defence of Leningrad. There had been some discussion by Kulik about arming the T-34 with a 107mm gun, but such a tank gun did not exist and would have required a very large turret. Kotin developed two KV-3 prototypes, the second retaining the basic KV-1 design but with an improved turret layout. The need for a new engine that was not available led to the cancellation of both designs.

The steady up-armouring of the KV-1 between 1941 and 1942 meant that it was simply not mobile enough to operate alongside the faster T-34. While the KV-1s were gathered into assault brigades to support the infantry, a heavy tank was still needed to support the mobile units. This problem was not really resolved until the introduction of the T-34 armed with a 85mm gun and the heavy IS tank.

The only interim solution was to make a lighter and therefore faster version of the KV-1. This led to the KV-1-S (S: *skorostnoy*, or speed) which was given a smaller and thinner turret as well as lighter road wheels. Overall, the armour was reduced, with the front given just 60mm. A much-needed improved clutch and gearbox was installed, as were improvements to engine lubrication and cooling. This gave the KV-1-S a road speed of 40km/h. It went into production in August 1943, but as it was no better armed than the T-34/76 only 1,379 were built before it was terminated in late 1943. Some KV-1-S were converted into flamethrowers using the ATO-42, becoming the KV-8S. Two prototypes of an upgraded KV-8S known as the KV-8M were produced equipped with two flamethrowers.

That year while work was done to develope the heavy IS tank and various large-calibre self-propelled weapons using the KV chassis, a turret with an 85mm gun was also fitted to a KV hull. This stopgap was designated the KV-85, but just 148 were built.

In the opening stages of the war many of the KV-2s photographed were derelict at the roadside, having either broken down or thrown a track, where they were found by bemused Germans. Some, though, do show combat damage, indicating they had fought as best they could against a much more mobile and flexible enemy.

The 12-ton turret on the KV-2 was enormous requiring side handrails for the crew to climb to the roof hatches. On this example a tow cable has been attached to the eyelet on the glacis, but shifting over 50 tons of tank would not have been easy. An early model T-26 light tank is to the left.

Two KV-2s left derelict on the road by their unit. The nearest has 'I Kompanie' scrawled on the side of the turret, the victors having already laid claim to it. This view shows to good effect the 152mm M1938/40 howitzer, which was provided with thirty-six rounds.

Another tank belonging to the same unit. Like the others, its turret is reversed.

It is not clear if this KV-2 was in a hull-down position to guard an airfield, or whether it simply sank in the soft ground. The discarded tow cable at the front implies it drowned in the soil. An elderly Soviet biplane has also been abandoned in the background.

Horse-drawn German baggage wagons pass a KV-2 left under a tree on the roadside. The turret could not be traversed unless the tank was on level ground, which severely restricted its ability to fight off-road.

Men from the Luftwaffe come to examine their handy work. When attacked by dive-bombers KV-2 crews had little option but to abandon ship. In this instance one of the crew did not make it and was killed on the glacis. The tank has thrown its right-hand track, which has gathered in front of the sprocket.

A close-up of the same tank, showing that something has torn the hull open buckling the side armour.

This side view shows an impact hole between the first and second return rollers. It was this that severed the track. The gun suffered damage as it has been holed.

The inspection team could not help but take one last photograph of themselves atop the stricken beast.

How 50 tons of KV-2 ended upside down is hard to imagine. The most ready explanation is that it has been shunted off a road and down the bank to the left. Like many KV tanks, the tow cable had been deployed.

During Operation Barbarossa the German Army was far from completely mechanised. These men are advancing using horses, horse-drawn wagons and bicycles. German cyclists take a moment to pose with the imposing bulk of a KV-2. The driver's visor is open so it is unlikely it was under fire when the crew gave up on it.

Not the most dignified of positions to be caught in by your comrades while inspecting the interior of a KV-2. The enormous gun could only be fired when stationary. Once more, note the presence of the attached tow cable.

This KV-2 put up a fight before succumbing. Three impact marks can be seen just to the right of the hull machine gun and on the right-hand side of the main gun mantlet. One KV-2 was recorded being hit over seventy times without its armour being penetrated.

Another roadside casualty. The left-hand track is severed.

Slewed into a ditch, three Germans assess their prize.

Blocking the road, this tank has caused some interest. The KV-2, like the KV-1, had a machine gun in the rear of the turret. The ball mounting can be seen to the left of the turret access door.

While a sound concept, the downfall of the KV-2 was its weight and mechanical unreliability. It suffered exactly the same clutch and transmission problems as the KV-1, which were exacerbated by the extra tonnage.

The last of the KV-2s saw action defending the approaches to Moscow. It had been intended for a direct-fire support, bunker busting role, but it never really got to fulfil this function. When KV production moved from Leningrad the KV-2 was discontinued.

Chapter Six

T-34

By 1941 the Red Army had in its possession a tank that was vastly superior to all its other designs with the partial exception of the KV-1. It first appeared the year before and was technically more advanced than Hitler's panzers. The only drawback for the Red Army was that when the war commenced it did not have many of them, and those it did have were suffering teething problems and needed time to be fine-tuned. This was a luxury they did not have.

This meant that the world-famous T-34 medium tank, along with the T-26 and BT-7, became one of the most-photographed tank wrecks on the Eastern Front. While the latter two types were photographed largely out of contempt and the T-28 and T-35 were photographed as lumbering novelties, the Germans must have taken their photos of the T-34 with a mixed sense of relief and amazement at how incompetently the Soviets had handled this modern-looking tank.

Like the other Soviet tank types, the T-34 was found abandoned in the most ridiculous of places, stranded in the middle of swamps, piled into each other, rear ended and even upside down. It was self-evident from these scenarios that the crews had little idea of what they were doing. This would change as the war progressed and the T-34's problems were ironed out, but in the meantime growing numbers of T-34s joined all the other tank wrecks on the Eastern Front.

During the 1930s tank designer Mikhail Koshkin began work on a new tank to replace the T-26 and BT. He suggested to Defence Commissar Voroshilov that to mark the 1934 state decree that had authorised the major expansion of the Red Army's armoured forces it be dubbed the T-34. Although working on a number of other designs, he envisaged a medium tank that would only run on tracks.

Two prototypes were completed by January 1940 and Koshkin, determined to prove the robustness of his design, drove them all the way from Kharkov to present them to Red Army officials in Moscow. They were then sent to Finland to test the 76.2mm gun on captured Finnish bunkers. Additional firing tests were conducted in Minsk and the prototypes were then sent back to Kharkov via Kiev. During February and March 1940 the T-34 prototypes covered a round trip of 2,280 miles.

The production T-34 Model 1940 came off the Kharkov factory floor in September 1940. Unfortunately, after his winter test drive Koshkin developed pneumonia and died at the end of the month. His colleague, Alexander Morozov, took over. Regrettably, due to problems with gun manufacture, the M1940 was armed with the inadequate short 76.2mm L-11 Model 1938 rifled gun with a length of 30.5 calibres. The T-34 carried 77 main gun rounds, though this was increased to 100 on the Model 1943.

This was a disaster because it meant the bulk of the T-34s started the war on the Eastern Front with a less effective gun, with predictable results. The following year a few were fitted with the 57mm ZiS-4 long-barrelled high-velocity gun, which could engage lightly armoured targets at a longer range.

The 76.2mm F-32 used to arm the KV-1 had better armour-piercing qualities than the L-11 because of its longer barrel. By the end of 1940 the former had been improved without authorisation to create the F-34 with 42 calibres, which was vastly superior to the L-11. The first T-34s armed with the F-34 and known as the Model 1941 appeared at Kharkov in February 1941. These were issued to company and platoon commanders and their enhanced hitting power was confirmed resisting the German invasion.

As word spread that the tankers did not want any more T-34s armed with the L-11, the Main Defence Committee officially authorised the F-34 as the standard T-34 tank weapon in August 1941. Firing the BT-350A, the standard Soviet armour piercing round at the beginning of the war, it could penetrate the Panzer III and cope with the Panzer IV Ausf F with 50mm of frontal armour at most ranges. With the introduction of the Tiger and Panther tanks the balance shifted because the F-34 could not penetrate their frontal armour at regular combat ranges. This was only remedied with the appearance of the T-34/85 armed with a 85mm gun in mid-1944.

The T-34 chassis utilised the Christie system, but instead of four pairs it had five pairs of road wheels (with a gap between the second and third) either side. Each was independently mounted and transversely swung on an interior vertical coil spring. Like the Christie M1928 and the BT tanks, the T-34 did not have return rollers. The drive sprockets were mounted at the back driving round the skeleton-type manganese steel tracks employing central guide horns that engaged alternate track links.

The most notable innovation on the T-34 was undoubtedly its wide tracks, which measured 483mm. This spread the ground pressure meaning that the T-34 did not exceed 0.7kg–0.75kg per cm. In contrast, American, British and German tanks exerted some 0.95kg–1kg per cm. The tracks were held together by dry track pins which were pushed back into place by a curved wiper plate welded on either side of the hull to the rear facing the upper track run. This system facilitated the swift removal of damaged track links or shoes and made life a lot easier for crews in combat when time was of the essence.

Unlike the Soviet's earlier tanks, the T-34's hull had sloped sides which overhung the upper track run. It was manufactured from homogeneous rolled-steel plate and electro welded together. The armour was 45mm at the front and sides and 20mm on the top. The glacis plate, 45mm thick, was set at a 60-degree angle with just two openings, one for the driver's hatch and one for the ball-mounted hull machine gun. The angle of the T-34's armour gave it the equivalent protection of 75mm of vertical armour. This made the T-34 almost invulnerable in 1941.

The power-to-weight ratio on the 28-ton tank was first class, thanks to the V-type four-stroke twelve-cylinder water-cooled diesel engine, which generated 493bhp at 1,800rpm. This gave the T-34 a top road speed of 54km/h and 10km/h cross-country. The less flammable diesel engine also increased the combat range to 464km compared with those tanks with petrol engines.

While the T-34 was a first-class design, it started the war with transmission problems, an inadequate gun, shortages of ammunition and fuel as well as very poor crew training. The result was that most of the early production T-34s were swiftly lost during the German invasion.*

* For more on the development and combat performance of the T-34 see the author's *Images of War Special: T-34 The Red Army's Legendary Medium Tank*, also published by Pen & Sword.

This German is standing by the remains of a battered T-34/76 Model 1940. The gun barrel has been bent out of shape and there is damage to the mantlet.

This T-34/76B or Model 1941 has a welded turret with the single large turret hatch.

A Model 1941 abandoned on the road. Early in the war the T-34 was prone to mechanical problems leading to breakdowns.

German mechanics examining a new T-34/76B Model 1941 with the rolled plate turret and one-piece hatch. They may be trying to start it as the side tool box is open as well as the rear engine cover.

A brand-new-looking T-34 – the tow cable draped over the side of the hull suggests it had broken down.

From their odd positioning these three T-34s were caught by German heavy artillery or bombers. The tank nearest the camera shows evidence that it burned as the tyres are missing.

A Model 1941 caught on the open road. The grisly remains of the crew rests on the ground just in front of the tank.

A close-up of the same tank. The tell-tale ash around the wheels is all that remains of the rubber tyres, but otherwise outwardly this Model 1941 looks undamaged.

Two Germans pose with a smashed T-34. The force of whatever destroyed the tank blew off one of the exhausts.

An abandoned Model 1940 T-34/76. This was the very first version armed with the short L-11 76.2mm mounted in a very distinctive cast cradle. This version was produced with both cast and welded turrets.

A strange place to read a book. The heavy one-piece hatch was not popular with the crews despite being designed to offer the commander some protection when opened up. It was replaced on subsequent models with twin circular hatches for the commander and the gunner, which were nicknamed 'Mickey Mouse' ears.

Two stranded T-34s and a BT tank. It looks as if they attempted to wade the pond only to drown their engines. Water and tanks are not a good combination, either the crews did not know that or they were desperate.

Everyone likes to 'rubberneck' at the scene of an accident. No one has seen fit to warn the soldier smoking on the left that the ground is likely to be soaked in diesel. This photograph was taken in late 1941 as most of the men are wearing greatcoats. The T-34 weighed 26 tons so it would have taken a considerable explosion to flip it.

This German despatch rider seated on a Model 1941/1942 T-34/76 appears to be examining a tank round. This version has a cast rather than rolled plate turret.

Model 1941 or 1942 with two of its dead crew members.

The first production model of the T-34 known as the Model 1940. Although powered by a diesel engine that was less flammable than petrol, most photographs of early T-34 wrecks show clear evidence of fire.

German troops examine the later Model 1943, also known as the T-34/76D. This featured a cast hexagonal turret and this particular example seems to have been captured intact.

The unfortunate tanker in the foreground had fled up the road and away from his stricken tank before he was shot down. If he had reached the ditch a few seconds sooner he might have lived.

One for the family album. A soldier balances on the barrel of a discarded T-34. The other two tanks have shunted each other.

These Germans are surveying a T-34/76 Model 1941. The vehicle appears spick and span suggesting it saw little if any action.

By familiarising yourself with enemy tanks it made it slightly easier to face them when active. The T-34, though, soon turned into the Wehrmacht's nemesis.

This tank has the cheaper metal-rimmed road wheels which made for an extremely uncomfortable and noisy ride for the crew. Wartime shortages imposed this limitation on some of the factories building the T-34. As usual, the tank looks intact.

Not the best way to climb into the driver's position of a T-34/76B. This tank looks almost brand new with barely a scratch on it.

A prime example of poor driver training.

A T-34/76 stuck fast in the mud. One of the exhaust pipes and its armoured covering is missing.

Chapter Seven

Panzer III

At the start of Operation Barbarossa the Panzerkampfwagen III, or Panzer III, constituted the most numerous German-built tank and was therefore photographed a lot by both sides. It formed the heart of Hitler's panzer divisions in the early stages of the invasion of the Soviet Union, but it could not cope with the Soviet KV-1 and T-34. Fortunately for the panzertruppen, the Red Army tank crews did not initially know how the get the best from their machines. As a result, their performance against the panzers was chaotic and ended in disaster.

Having gained experience with their early Panzer I and II, by the mid-1930s the Germans had begun to draw up their requirements for heavier main battle tanks. General Heinz Guderian's intention was to have two basic types with different functions. The first would have an anti-tank role and be armed with a high-velocity gun, the second would be a support tank equipped with a large-calibre gun that could deliver a high-explosive shell. One could deal with enemy tanks the other with enemy infantry and fortifications. These would be designated the Panzer III and Panzer IV. The plan was that the panzer battalions would have three companies in the tank-to-tank role and one company with support tanks.

The first of these medium tanks emerged as the Panzer Mk III, which was to be armed with a 50mm tank gun. In its day this would have been a large weapon and certainly bigger than the 45mm gun that armed most Soviet tanks. Unfortunately, the standard German infantry anti-tank gun at the time was a 37mm and in the name of standardisation the first models of Panzer III were armed with this. Fortuitously, the large turret ring design was retained, which meant that the tank could be up-gunned with the 50mm gun once it became available. The specifications called for a tank weighting 14.7 tons, which was never kept to, and an upper limit of 23.6 tons to permit it to use German road bridges without mishap. Depending on the model, the Panzer III ranged from 19.5 to 23 tons.

The initial prototypes were produced in 1936 with Daimler-Benz as the main contractor. The early models, the Ausf A, B, C and D, were part of an ongoing development process and were only built in small numbers. The Ausf E became the first true production version and was accepted in September 1939. A Panzer III production group was then set up utilising other manufacturers. Just under 100 Ausf E were available for the invasion of Poland and 350 took part in the invasion of France in May 1940. These forces, though, included some of the other earlier versions. During this operation a number of Panzer IIIs were lost to various causes.

The Panzer III's fighting compartment was reasonably spacious and the commander's cupola on the turret top gave good all-round visibility. It soon became apparent that the 37mm gun and the 30mm of frontal armour were woefully inadequate. The new Krupp 50mm KwK L/42 gun was used to arm the later Ausf E up to the J versions from April 1940 onwards. While this low-velocity gun was not entirely satisfactory, it could fire high-explosive shells.

Throughout its career the Panzer III was steadily improved upon as combat experience highlighted its shortcomings. Notably, the Ausf H had extra armour bolted to the turret and hull, while the tracks were widened to help cope with the atrocious muddy and wintry conditions in the Soviet Union. For ease of production and to help the crews, the complicated and difficult to maintain ten-speed gearbox was replaced by a simpler six-speed manual change.

The Panzer III ranged from the Ausf A to N (minus I and K), plus numerous specialised variants that included armoured recovery, command and flamethrower vehicles. In its final incarnation the Panzer III was used in a support role (originally intended for the Panzer IV), designated the Ausf N this was armed with a low-velocity short-barrelled 75mm gun, which had been used on the early StuG III and Panzer IV. By 1943, despite the upgrades, the Panzer III was obsolete as a combat tank and at this stage 6,100 had been built.

In 1941 there were just under 1,500 Panzer IIIs in service and they proved quite successful in the opening stages of the invasion of the Soviet Union. On 20 June 1941 Hitler had seventeen panzer divisions poised to attack the Red Army, of which eleven were equipped with the Panzer III. Each light-armoured company had been issued with its full complement of 17 Panzer IIIs, which meant of total of 960 Panzer III Ausf E to Js.

Alarmingly, the Red Army's new KV-1 and T-34 tanks proved immune to the 50mm KwK L/42 gun. This had to be upgraded to the KwK L/60, a high-velocity version used on the Ausf J to M, but even this soon proved inadequate against increasing Soviet tank armour. It was of little value against the KV-1 or T-34 in frontal engagements.

In the first year of the fighting in Russia and North Africa around 1,400 Panzer IIIs were lost. In June 1942 at the beginning of the summer campaign on the Eastern Front there were about 500 Panzer IIIs armed with the 50mm KwK L/42 available and some 600 Panzer IIIs mounting the 50mm KwK39 L/60. At the start of Hitler's Kursk offensive a year later Army Groups Centre and South could still muster 141 with the L/42 and 432 with the L/60. This meant that wrecked Panzer IIIs were regularly photographed by Red Army cameramen right up until the end of 1943. Typically, the Panzer III was pictured knocked out and having lost its tracks.

The Panzer III could best be likened to a hard-working donkey, which ultimately had to be put out to pasture. When that happened the highly reliable chassis was turned over to StuG III assault-gun production. This proved vastly more successful than the gun tank.

The Panzer III provided the backbone of Hitler's tank force on the Eastern Front during the first few years. Its armour proved too thin and its gun not powerful enough. This one has taken a round straight through the turret. Some of the crew got out as the side hull escape hatch is open.

A Red Army lorry speeds past a Panzer III on the roadside. The left-hand side of the turret appears damaged and there is an impact mark on the gun mantlet.

Panzer III '614' from the 2nd Panzer Division has taken a battering. The front drive sprocket is missing and the tracks have come off. Also a hole has been punched through the tool box on the back of the tank.

Bearing the number '333', this scorched tank suffered an internal explosion which took off the turret roof. A rear idler is missing and the tyres on the return rollers and wheels have melted with the heat of the subsequent blaze.

Another mangled Panzer III that has been punched full of holes. The turret armour just to the right of the gun mantlet has shattered.

Soviet officers and men examine the burnt-out remains of a Panzer III Ausf J. The turret side hatches are open suggesting some of the crew at least may have escaped. Interestingly, the muzzle of the barrel appears to be obstructed.

This appears to be the same tank photographed from a different angle. Note the brick on the tank's left-hand mudguard and the same scoring marks on the lower part of the glacis.

Stuck in a crater, this Panzer III for some reason has been taped off from the road. The smoking crewman seems fairly relaxed. The passing onlookers are riding in SdKfz 251 armoured half-tracks.

The man to the right leaning on the track guard is taking notes indicating that these men are from Red Army intelligence.

A well-camouflaged Panzer III found stuck in the mud in the woods. The upturned rifle to the left of the tank shows fatalities were incurred.

Derelict panzers were often cannibalised for spares, such as this Panzer III which looks to have been pulled apart.

Two Panzer IIIs undergo maintenance as German mountain troops trudge by.

The derelict remains of Panzer III 'I I I' – the turret bustle or storage bin has been shot off.

This atmospheric shot sums up the fate of the Panzer III on the road to Moscow in the winter of 1941–2. Nonetheless, during the summer of 1943 the German Army still had 740 that fought at Kursk.

The KV-1 to the left with supporting infantry easily outgunned the Panzer III, as did the T-34.

Another careless driver – an early model Panzer III that has lost a track and almost ended up in someone's vegetable patch.

A broken track shoe instantly exposed the repair team to enemy fire and usually led to a mad scramble to get back in the tank at the first sign of fighting.

A Panzer III Ausf E or F. Although the tank quickly proved inadequate on the Eastern Front, by mid-1942 the Panzerwaffe were still fielding 1,100 of them.

It is not entirely clear if this Panzer III Ausf M is on fire or laying down smoke. The commander visible in the turret indicates the latter.

Mangled Panzer IIIs destroyed on the Eastern Front. In the first year of the fighting in Russia and North Africa about 1,400 Panzer IIIs were lost.

Chapter Eight

Panzer IV

Throughout much of the war on the Eastern Front, the Panzer IV provided the backbone of the panzerwaffe, especially once it was up-gunned with a decent anti-tank gun. Along with the StuG III, it bore the brunt of the fighting and as a result thousands were knocked out. It has the accolade of being the only German tank to remain in continuous production throughout the Second World War. In addition, it was in production longer than any Allied tank with the exception of the T-34. It also proved to be the best German medium tank – the Panzer V Panther, classified a heavy medium tank, was let down by reliability and availability.

The Panzer IV shared many of the design features of the Panzer III, being robust, well made and giving a good cross-country performance. Also its large turret ring ensured it could take more powerful guns than the Panzer III, which enabled it to stay in service until the very end of the conflict. Its development commenced in 1935 along with the Panzer III, when the Germans decided that their main battle tanks would have two roles, acting either as a dedicated gun tank or as a high-explosive firing support tank. The Panzer IV was initially allotted the latter role – which turned out to be a serious mistake.

As a result, the Panzer III and Panzer IV were developed alongside each other. Their specifications were quite similar in terms of layout and suspension. However, while the first acted as Hitler's beast of burden until abandoned in favour of assault-gun production, the latter remained Hitler's rock throughout the war. At first the weapon selected for the Panzer IV was the high-explosive-firing short-barrelled low-velocity 75mm KwK37 L/24 gun. Essentially, this made the early versions of the Panzer IV little more than self-propelled artillery.

By 1939 the Panzer IV Ausf D was available for the Polish and French campaigns. Although slightly larger than the Panzer III, being longer and higher, it had a comparable shape. Notably, the turret traverse was by an electric motor, while the Panzer III traverse was manual. Like the Panzer III, it had a commander's cupola offering good all-round vision. The engine was also mounted to the rear and was the same as that of the Panzer III. Suspension consisted of four coupled bogies on each side with eight wheels, sprung by leaf springs, with four return rollers above them.

The Panzer III had six wheels either side with three return rollers – making it very easy to differentiate them. The drive ran forward to a front-mounted gearbox and the drive sprockets on both tanks.

Early combat experience showed that while the Panzer IV was a good design, its armour was too thin to enable it to support the Panzer III and it lacked any real advantages over its opponents. The subsequent Ausf E had thicker armour on the turret and glacis plus a new cupola. Nonetheless, the role of the Panzer IV remained very limited and it was not a true battle tank, nor was it intended to be. There were 438 Panzer IV Ausf B–Fs serving with Hitler's panzer divisions when he attacked the Soviet Union in June 1941, so it was a very common sight.

Then came an important game-changer. From the F model onwards the short 75mm gun was replaced with the vastly superior long-barrelled 75mm KwK40 L/43 tank gun, which first appeared in early 1942. It could fire armour-piercing rounds to a considerable range. This gave the Panzer IV a much-needed new lease of life and enabled it to take on almost any tank, including the T-34. The appearance of this tank in both Russia and in North Africa made a considerable difference to German fortunes on the battlefield. Understandably, the Red Army became desperate to get hold of an up-gunned Panzer IV Ausf F2.

From the Ausf G onwards the Panzer IV had an even more powerful 75mm gun, the KwK40 L/48. The G was very similar to the F, but with minor improvements, including thicker side armour. The subsequent Ausf H was the most produced and therefore the most common on the Eastern Front. It featured thicker armour, an improved transmission and a new idler design.

The build-up of the better armed Panzer IV was relatively slow. In late June 1942 at the start of the summer offensive in the Soviet Union there were only about 170 Ausf F2s and Gs on the Eastern Front. However, this number had increased to 841 at the start of the Kursk offensive the following summer, which greatly helped offset the panzer divisions still heavy reliance on the inadequate Panzer III.

The last model of the Panzer IV was the Ausf J, which appeared in 1944. Due to a lack of raw materials, many of the frills of the earlier models were dispensed with, most notably the electric turret traverse much to the displeasure of the gunners. Nevertheless, it remained essentially the same tank that had started the Second World War five years before – only with a better gun and a significant change in role. Like the Panzer III, the IV chassis was also the basis for numerous different types of specialised variants. These included assault guns, tank destroyers and self-propelled guns. By 1945 over 8,500 Panzer IVs had been built. A total of 6,100 of these were destroyed on the Eastern Front, which meant it became one of the most photographed panzer wrecks.

The smashed remains of a Panzer IV. This was the most common German tank but the initial variants had armour that was too thin and a gun that was only designed to support infantry by firing high explosive. The hull front plate has come right off and the glacis is twisted and buckled.

An early model Panzer IV Ausf E armed with the short 75mm support gun abandoned in the snow. It appears to have slid off a road and down a bank.

A Panzer IV Ausf G wreck photographed in the aftermath of the Battle of Kursk in July 1943. Over 840 Panzer IVs were massed for Hitler's ill-fated Operation Citadel, which expended the last of the Panzerwaffe's strength.

Soviet soldiers pick through assorted debris left by a German column on the Russian steppe. Two Panzer IVs lie abandoned among the detritus, on the nearest the road wheels have frozen solid.

A damaged Panzer IV Ausf F2 – it has lost two road wheels and the track has been severed. The blackening along the hull means the tank and its crew burned after being hit. The trackless tank behind it is an American M3 Stuart supplied under Lend Lease. Armed with just a 37mm gun, it came off worse against this F2. The Soviets disliked American tanks because of their high silhouettes and thin armour.

This abandoned vehicle appears to be some sort of Bergepanzer IV armoured recovery vehicle or engineer/munitions carrier. It is not clear if the object to the right is the remains of a turret.

This Panzer IV has been completely ripped apart. The whole of the superstructure has moved forward with the force of the blast.

An explosion tore the superstructure clean of this Panzer IV. The left-hand track is also missing judging from the exposed idler.

Souvenir hunters scour the remains of a Panzer IV. After a tank burned there would be little if anything of use or value left remaining.

Panzer IV Ausf G '649' knocked out on the Eastern Front. The glacis plate has been penetrated, killing the driver instantly. As the commander's hatch is flung open the commander and the gunner may have escaped.

A Panzer IV lost on the streets of Budapest in 1945. Its 75mm gun is missing its muzzle brake.

A German horse column passing a Panzer IV blown to smithereens.

Wrecked Panzer III obstructing Panzer IV '610', the right-side track and sprocket are missing as is a portion of the track guard rendering it immobile. These two types of tanks were designed to work together in a tank-to-tank and infantry support role respectively.

An early Model Panzer IV in the Stalingrad area in 1942. This region would become a graveyard for all types of German armour.

Panzer IVs lost in the winter snows – this type of tank served as a gun tank from 1942 on the Eastern Front until the very end of the war.

Chapter Nine

Tiger

The famous or infamous Panzer VI Tiger heavy tank was designed to stand off and kill T-34s at great range. However, its debut on the Eastern Front was extremely inauspicious and its subsequent performance at Kursk was not enough to stave off defeat. Between 1942 and 1944 just 1,300 Tigers were produced, yet the Tiger I and II were photographed regularly on the Eastern Front. This was by virtue of them being impressive-looking tanks, but also because their weight made them very difficult to recover. If after an engagement the Germans did not possess the battlefield, rescuing damaged and stranded Tiger tanks was all but impossible.

The German requirement for a heavy breakthrough tank had first been developed in the late 1930s. This meant that the Tiger had already been designed and was unable to draw on the innovations of the T-34. In contrast, the German Panther tank was a new design in 1942 and was very influenced by the T-34, duplicating many of its innovative features.

What rapidly became clear with the early prototypes for the Tiger was that the T-34's 76.2mm gun made the proposal to use the Panzer IV 75mm L/48 gun obsolete. In addition, it meant that the Tiger's weight slowly crept up from 33 tons to 36 tons and then 45 tons. The latter was ordered in May 1941 with a proposal that it should mount a tank version of the 88mm anti-aircraft gun. This turned into a rushed job as it had to be ready for Hitler's birthday on 20 April 1942. Both Henschel and Porsche were instructed to produce competing prototypes that could be presented to Hitler.

The Henschel design was judged to be the best and manufacture was authorised to commence in August 1942. The production models exceeded the specified weight of 45 tons by 12 tons. The tank was designated the Panzerkampfwagen VI Tiger Ausf H – the Sonderk raftfahrzeug or Ordnance Number was SdKfz 181. The designation was subsequently changed to PzKpfw Tiger Ausf E in February 1944.

When it first appeared on the battlefield in late 1942 the Tiger I was a first-class design with its powerful 88mm gun and up to 100mm of armour. This made the 57-ton monster the most formidable tank in existence. Notably, it was the first

German tank to feature an overlapping road-wheel suspension. This had triple overlapping and interleaved steel disc wheels with solid rubber tyres. In the later model the wheels had steel tyres with internal springs, a design copied from the Soviets.

Despite its weight, the Tiger offered a surprisingly soft and stable ride. This was thanks to the eight independently sprung torsion bar axles each side. To fit them inside the hull they were staggered on the floor with the left-hand axles led forward and the right-hand axles trailed aft. The wheels could be fitted with wide tracks for combat and narrow ones for transportation; to fit the latter required removing the outer wheel from each suspension unit. While this suspension gave the crew a more comfortable ride, it came at a price. The interleaved wheels in the winter could become clogged and jammed with mud, snow and ice. The Red Army soon developed the tactic of timing its attacks for dawn to ensure German vehicles had been immobilised during the overnight freeze.

Tiger I production ran from August 1942 until August 1944, by which time from an order of 1,376 some 1,350 tanks had been delivered. Production peaked in April 1944 when 104 rolled out of the factory. The Tiger's weight meant that most road bridges could not bear it, so the first 496 Tigers were waterproofed to a depth of 13ft with snorkel breathing. The rest were produced able to wade through water to a maximum depth of 4ft. The Henschel Tiger was certainly the best-quality tank ever put into mass-production during the Second World War. But it was enormously expensive to build and labour intensive. Gigantic machine tools and jigs were required to assemble the hulls. Such lavish expenditure on a tank at a time when numbers were more important than quality is difficult to fathom.

Due to the vehicle's limited numbers, the Tiger battalions acted as independent units on the Eastern Front. These were then allotted to support panzer divisions for specific operations. Although the Tiger was a spearhead tank due to its relatively slow speed and size, its flanks always had to be protected by medium tanks. It had been hoped to add the Tiger to the basic organisation of the panzer divisions, but due to slow production, serviceability problems and attrition there were never enough available. The exception was the Waffen-SS, whose panzer divisions were some of the first units to receive the Tiger; these included the 1st SS Panzer Division Leibstandarte SS Adolf Hitler and the 2nd SS Panzer Division Das Reich.

The first commitment of the Tigers to battle was in Russia at Leningrad and in North Africa in Tunisia. This was not successful because of the pitifully small numbers involved which enabled enemy anti-tank gunners to get the better of them. The attack at Leningrad in 1942 was on terrain that the Tiger was woefully incapable of coping with. It fought best on the open steppe where its long-range gun could kill enemy tanks at a safe distance. Instead, it found itself driving in single file through dense Russian forests and swamps that could swallow a tank whole (and frequently did). The Soviet gunners defending the forest tracks were able to beat them off easily.

The Tiger's deadly main armament, the 88mm KwK36 L/56 gun, could penetrate 110mm of armour at 2,000m. The Soviets, though, soon identified one of the Tiger's key weak points, other than its mechanical reliability, the very slow turret traverse. This meant that once the T-34 had closed to within range it could outmanoeuvre and outshoot the Tiger. Undeterred by early setbacks, Hitler put great faith in both the Tiger I and Panther tanks in the summer of 1943, but again there were simply not enough to have any decisive impact on the outcome of the Battle of Kursk. It was a problem that was to plague the German Army for the rest of the war.

The Red Army understood the propaganda and morale value of photographing the slain Tiger. It was very important that its soldiers fully appreciated that the Tiger was not invincible and could be defeated. Thanks to the examples captured outside Leningrad and afterwards the Red Army was able to issue special defensive instructions to its men just before Kursk. Most Tigers photographed were either long abandoned or had been specially posed by the cameraman for maximum dramatic effect. Soviet soldiers took great pleasure in being photographed with both the Tiger I and II, which for all their engineering excellent did not prove to be war winners.

A Soviet soldier examining a battered Tiger I belonging to the Grossdeutschland Panzergrenadier Division. This division's panzer regiment included Tigers and Panthers at Kursk. It has the later style road wheels and has lost a track. Part of the Zimmerit coating has come off under the impact of an incoming round.

Another late-production Tiger lost on the Eastern Front – while an extremely powerful gun tank, its weight proved a problem making it difficult to recover. This one seems to have been abandoned.

The crew of this Tiger appear to be waiting for assistance – note the row of rocket launchers to their right. The tank has not been whitewashed making it stick out in the winter landscape.

The Tiger was vulnerable in close-quarter combat and certainly was not ideal for urban combat. Enemy tanks or tank-hunter teams would have crept up on this one. The 88mm gun barrel on '113' has been shot off and the right track has been thrown.

This derelict early production Tiger '121' is very new as it still has its factory finish of dark sand-yellow known as *dunkelgelb*. The only concession to winter camouflage is the snow on the glacis. The forward outer road wheel is missing.

Abandon ship. This tank it either on fire or laying down smoke.

A Tiger with its turret reversed which has been on the steppe for some time judging by its covering of snow. The Tiger excelled in open space such as this where its long-range gun gave it a great advantage over enemy tanks.

A T-34 tank and supporting infantry take a close look at their handiwork. The Tiger was exposed on this raised road and was probably caught from behind at close range. Again, it has not been camouflaged for the winter conditions.

The Tiger II was built in even fewer numbers than the Tiger I, so was treated as a novelty by the Red Army. This captured example is being used as a training aid or for intelligence purposes.

The front view of the same captured Tiger II – it looks undamaged suggesting it broke down.

A shattered Tiger I caught on the streets – it has no wheels indicating it had been cannibalised for spares or was being used as a static pillbox.

The Red Army laid on this display of captured German hardware which includes on the right a Tiger II, two Tiger Is and a couple of Panthers. On the left are Hungarian and Italian assault guns as well as a German Marder tank destroyer.

This Tiger II has been used for ballistic tests – impact marks are the results of 57mm, 85mm and 100mm guns. Incredibly, these have made little more than dents in the thick armour.

A wrecked Tiger II minus its gun barrel and nearside drive sprocket.

The final resting place for one of the very last Tiger Is on Berlin's Unter den Linden strasse, not far from the Brandenburg Gate, in 1945. It belonged to Panzer Battalion Müncheberg, part of Panzer Division Müncheberg, which was a division in name only. Even at the end of the war tank-wreck sightseeing was still a preoccupation with the Red Army.

Chapter Ten

Panther

Up until Operation Barbarossa in June 1941 the Panzer IV was the German Army's heaviest tank. Like the Panzer III, it soon proved inadequate in the face of the Soviet KV-1 and T-34. The Red Army's initial handling of the T-34 proved a complete disaster. Even so there was no hiding its superior armament, armour, speed and above all manoeuvrability (in the right hands). Overnight, Hitler's panzers were shown to be completely outdated, as were Stalin's T-26 and BT-7.

The Germans knew that they needed a medium tank that could mimic the key qualities of the T-34 and quickly. The only way Hitler was able to regain his technical superiority and ensure any parity with the Red Army's growing numbers of tanks was to introduce the Panzer V Panther heavy medium and the Panzer VI Tiger heavy tanks into service before the Allies developed anything comparable.

The impulse was to clone the T-34 but national pride coupled with a lack of certain raw materials thwarted such action. Nonetheless, when the specification was issued in January 1942 it included all the T-34's basic features. In April designs were submitted and the Maschinenfabrik Augsburg Nürnberg (MAN) version was selected, becoming the Pzkpfw V Panther (SdKfz 171).

The Panther, like the Tiger, had the dual advantage and disadvantage of using a complicated suspension with inter-leaved bogies sprung on torsion bars. While this gave a good ride cross-country, the bogies could clog up and freeze during the hard Russian winter thereby immobilising the tank. Also, as on the Tiger, it meant that maintenance of the wheels could be time consuming, because to get to the inner ones the outer ones had to be first removed.

Frustratingly for Hitler's Panzerwaffe, the first production Panther did not appear until January 1943. Even then it was not up to scratch and was far from combat ready, which made it vulnerable. With the help of Daimler-Benz it was intended that MAN would build 600 Panthers every month, but this ambitious target was never reached. The Panther being a wartime design inevitably suffered teething problems, which haunted it throughout its combat career. The first version, designated the Ausf D, at 43 tons put great stress on the interleaved disc wheels, the engine and transmission, plus engine cooling was insufficient. As a result, it regularly overheated and broke down and soon fell into the hands of the Red Army.

The Panther's hull interior had the conventional German layout, but with distinctive exterior sloping sides and a large sloping one-piece glacis plate with openings for the driver and hull machine gun. The third model, the Ausf G, only had the ball mount for the hull machine gun, with the driver relying on a periscope to navigate. The turret sides were likewise well sloped, though the interior was cramped, but the commander was served by an excellent cupola giving him good 360-degree vision on the battlefield. The thickly armoured gun mantlet had openings, for the main armament and smaller ones for the gunner's sight and the coaxial machine gun.

Hitler was insistent that the Panther be sent into action immediately rather than wait until it had been fine-tuned and was available in large numbers. Nor were the crews given adequate time to train and practise their tactics – many of the men were new recruits. This inevitably played right into the Red Army's hands. It was not long before they got hold of their first examples of the Panther. Just three battalions equipped with the Panther were first committed to combat in July 1943 during the Battle of Kursk, where it proved highly unreliable. There were still ongoing problems with the engine, transmission and suspension and most of the Panthers after leaving the railhead broke down before they even reached the front. Several caught fire because of overheating.

The poor crew training also helped the Soviets counter this new armoured monster. At Kursk crossing the Berezovyi Ravine proved a complete and utter shambles with the Panthers unable to get out once they had rolled in. Chaos ensued. Within 5 days of the German attack opening at Kursk they had lost 125 Panthers from a force of 200, though a large number of these were recoverable and repairable. When the dust cleared the Red Army had captured at least seven and these were hauled off for examination and testing. The three things that proved really successfully on the Panther were its sloped armour, powerful gun and wide tracks.

After the Ausf D there were two further models, the A and G, which improved on some of the earlier tiresome shortcomings. It would appear fighting on the Eastern Front and in Italy identified two particular weaknesses with the armour. One was that the bottom of the mantlet could act as a shot trap, which led to damage of the main gun or the turret jamming. The other was that the driver's vision hatch in the glacis presented a potential weak spot in the frontal armour.

While some photos of Panthers on the Eastern Front do clearly show severe damage to the mantlet, none have emerged with the driver's hatch shot in. Therefore, it is not entirely clear if the driver's vision port was omitted on the Ausf G because it presented a weak point or simply for ease of manufacture. It is possible that it was a combination of both. In late summer of 1944 some Panther Ausf Gs were fitted with a mantlet that eliminated the under curve with the installation of a prominent forward-angled projection. This was intended to flick enemy rounds away from the turret.

Despite being over engineered, the Panther with its powerful 75mm KwK42 L/70 gun and thick sloped frontal armour could stand off and kill Soviet tanks with little danger to its crew. It was liked by the Panzerwaffe and considered by some as the best panzer of the war. Hitler, though, had a great propensity for throwing them away at inopportune moments, so arguably the Panther could have achieved more given time. The Panther did not save the day at Kursk and its greatest contribution was covering the German retreat from southern Ukraine. In the face of Stalin's Operation Bagration the following year the insufficient Panthers could only cover the retreat from Byelorussia and blunt the Red Army's advance before Warsaw.

By the end of the war almost 6,000 had been built, but by 1943 what Hitler needed was ever larger numbers of panzers rather than highly engineered designs that were costly and time-consuming to build. Nonetheless, the Panther was the third most-produced German armoured vehicle after the StuG III and Panzer IV so was a very common sight on the battlefield. The Red Army photographed the Panther across the length and breadth of the Eastern Front, usually after it had been destroyed. Some of the very first images were taken just after Kursk when the Panther was a novelty to Soviet tank crews and anti-tank gunners. Those taken on the battlefield inevitably meant that the Soviets were soon made aware of its secrets.

The Panther tank was first blooded at the Battle of Kursk in July 1943 and this was the result – heavy losses. Soviet troops examine the remains of Panther Ausf D '312'. They do not seem terribly impressed.

This Ausf D, belonging to the 52nd Panzer Battalion, was also lost at Kursk. The vehicle to the left is an SdKfz 263 radio car. Although based on an armoured car, it was not designed to be a fighting vehicle.

A Panther Ausf D from the 51st Panzer Battalion photographed after Kursk. The Panther proved chronically unreliable and many broke down before they even reached their jump-off point.

The rear view of the same tank which has lost one of its exhaust pipes. Another Panther can just be made out on the left.

Soviet infantry explore the remains of a Kursk Panther. The turret and turret ring have both been torn off.

Captured Panther Ausf D '433' – Heinz Guderian was annoyed that Hitler insisted on utilising the Panther at Kursk before it was combat ready. Only three battalions were used, which was not enough, and Hitler threw away the element of surprise.

When the Red Army counterattacked following Hitler's failed Kursk offensive this Ausf D was destroyed outside Kharkov in August 1944. From the state of the road wheels it has clearly been consumed by fire.

The Panther had an extremely powerful 75mm gun which meant it excelled in fighting on the open steppe. Soviet tankers had to close with the Panther and Tiger as quickly as they could to engage on anything like equal terms. These three look burnt out – this may have been done deliberately to stop them falling into enemy hands.

A broken down Panther Ausf A which has been given a fairly poor coat of whitewash.

Smiling Soviet soldiers go souvenir hunting. The corrugated surface on this Panther is due to the anti-magnetic paste known as Zimmerit. The column is made up of a variety of other tanks and armoured fighting vehicles, including a Hummel self-propelled gun.

The final model of Panther was designated the Ausf G. This is a late build as it has the new mantlet designed to eliminate a shot trap under the barrel and no Zimmerit coating. The latter was discontinued for fear the paste was flammable, however, the main reason was that it was time consuming to apply.

A monument to the liberation of Budapest in 1945. This Panther is believed to have belonged to the 13th Panzer Division.

The same tank minus it turret and road wheels.

The remains of a Panther turret used as a strongpoint. By this stage of the war mobility counted for little in the face of the Red Army's relentless tide.

This Panther turret went down fighting. It is surrounded by about fifty spent shell cases.

Having saved their Panther, this crew highlighted the amount of punishment their tank took. A total of sixteen impact marks have been circled on the front so they are clearly very lucky to be still alive. It may explain why they look shaken.

Further Reading

Tucker-Jones, Anthony, *Images of War: The Panzer III Hitler's Beast of Burden* (Pen & Sword Military, 2017)

Tucker-Jones, Anthony, illustrated by Hemingway, David Lee, *Images of War Special: The Panzer IV Hitler's Rock* (Pen & Sword Military, 2017)

Tucker-Jones, Anthony, illustrated by Hemingway, David Lee, *Images of War Special: The Panther Tank Hitler's T-34 Killer* (Pen & Sword Military, 2016)

Tucker-Jones, Anthony, *Images of War: German Assault Guns and Tank Destroyers 1940–1945* (Pen & Sword Military, 2016)

Tucker-Jones, Anthony, illustrated by Hemingway, David Lee, *Images of War Special: T-34 The Red Army's Legendary Medium Tank* (Pen & Sword Military, 2015)

Tucker-Jones, Anthony, illustrated by Delf, Brian, *Images of War Special: Tiger I & Tiger II* (Pen & Sword Military, 2013)

Tucker-Jones, Anthony, *Images of War: Armoured Warfare on the Eastern Front* (Pen & Sword Military, 2011)